THIS IS ME!

INSPIRING WORDS

Edited By Debbie Killingworth

First published in Great Britain in 2022 by:

Young Writers
Remus House
Coltsfoot Drive
Peterborough
PE2 9BF
Telephone: 01733 890066
Website: www.youngwriters.co.uk

Book Design by Ashley Janson

Softback ISBN 978-1-80015-813-9

Printed and bound in the UK by BookPrintingUK
Website: www.bookprintinguk.com
YB0496K

FOREWORD

For Young Writers' latest competition This Is Me, we asked primary school pupils to look inside themselves, to think about what makes them unique, and then write a poem about it! They rose to the challenge magnificently and the result is this fantastic collection of poems in a variety of poetic styles.

Here at Young Writers our aim is to encourage creativity in children and to inspire a love of the written word, so it's great to get such an amazing response, with some absolutely fantastic poems. It's important for children to focus on and celebrate themselves and this competition allowed them to write freely and honestly, celebrating what makes them great, expressing their hopes and fears, or simply writing about their favourite things. This Is Me gave them the power of words. The result is a collection of inspirational and moving poems that also showcase their creativity and writing ability.

I'd like to congratulate all the young poets in this anthology, I hope this inspires them to continue with their creative writing.

CONTENTS

Ripley Junior School, Ripley

Elliot Haynes-Ward (9)	67
Ella T (9)	68
Annabel Brown (9)	69
Daisy Hinett (9)	70
Olivia Walder (9)	71
Corey Hall (9)	72
Molly Monks (9)	73
Isabella-Rose Weightman (9)	74
Blake Davis (9)	75
Max Fletcher (9)	76
Leo Delrosso (9)	77
Poppy Jarvis (9)	78
Scarlett-Leigh Starr (9)	79
Isobel Waller-Skermer (9)	80
Ashton Brunt (9)	81
Iona-Lilly Edwards (9)	82
Joshua Annable (9)	83

Sheffield High School For Girls (Junior), Broomhill

Clemence Moran-Healy (9)	84
Phoebe Mary Doig (9)	86
Julide Senior (9)	87
Orla Hague (8)	88
Ava Rogers (7)	89
Summer Kelly (9)	90
Aanya Saxena (10)	91
Pranathi Naveen (8)	92
Ariana Ramlakhan (9)	93
Neha Varghese (9)	94
Matilda Wild (9)	95
Aaruthe Srirakaran (8)	96
Trudy Ludlam (8)	97
Isabella Taylor (9)	98
Natsumi Wong (9)	99
Yuge Wang (9)	100
Isobel Riddle (9)	101
Sara Nasim (10)	102
Habiba Gabr (8)	103
Mimi Taylor (7)	104
Isabella Cancello (10)	105
Anya Mangat (8)	106
Lilia Maraqa (10)	107
Isabelle Flemons (9)	108
Carlotta Bailey (8)	109
Amelia Somasundram (8)	110
Riha Ganesh (11)	111
Alicia Villalba Ramos (8)	112
Amelia Beck (9)	113
Anu Akilan	114
Emma Kong (7)	115
Phoebe Preston (7)	116
Kitty Sumner (9)	117
Aleesha Pillay (8)	118
Noor Akram (10)	119

St Peter's Church Of England Aided Junior School, Farnborough

Bella	120
Erica Atkinson (9)	121
Georgia Taylor (9)	122
Jemma Hoare (9)	123
Emma Cunningham (9)	124
Amelia Lynch (9)	125
Taya Offord (9)	126
Georgia O'Connor (9)	127
Jess Owen (9)	128
Mallory Earle (10)	129
Frankie Burge (9)	130
Elsie-Jayne Slevin (9)	131
Jason Adamik (9)	132
Georgia Kelly (9)	133
Isaac Morgan (10)	134
Zita L (9)	135
Freddie Hankin (9)	136
Evie Churchill (8)	137
Lucy Grenham (9)	138
Thomas Anderson (9)	139
James Prinsloo (8)	140
Erin Hammond (9)	141
Grace Harrison (9)	142
Sammy Ronald Stembridge (9)	143
Freya Sabatini (9)	144
Gabrielle Wilson (10)	145

THE POEMS

Rap About Aaminah

Hey everyone, listen yo,
Here are some things you should know about me.
My name? It's Aaminah yeah, ready to rap.
I'm as short as a mouse, *squeak, squeak!*
My hair is as dark as the night sky,
I'll make sure to give you a fright.
My eyes are brown like chocolate.
My favourite colour is yellow
Just like a banana as ripe as can be,
Ripe = right, and that is me,
I'll give you a smile when you see me,
I'm the best you can see.
I was born 10 years ago and a miracle happened.
I go to the best school Millbrook Combined School
But don't forget I'm in 6NH the best class,
Mrs Hussain is my teacher,
Miss Richards is the teaching assistant.
A-a-m-i-n-a-h that's how you spell my name.
Now you should remember me!

Aaminah Kiyani (10)
Millbrook Combined School, High Wycombe

Recipe To Me

How do you make me?
Mean as can be,
Rude like a gossiping bee,
Crash, bang, boom!
But that's not me!
Short like a sprouting tree,
I'm a hindrance you see,
Crash, bang, boom!
But that's not me!
Kinder than a teacher you see,
Artistic that's me,
As tall as a twisted tangled tree,
Always listening to music,
Yes, that's me!
Black holes for eyes!
But what else could I be?
Reading that's it!
I'm always reading somewhere,
On a roof, in a car or even in the trees,
I can't be seen anywhere without a book
beside me,

Put it in the mixture and you will see,
Crash, bang, boom!
Now that's me.

Kiarnae Ongiagha (10)
Millbrook Combined School, High Wycombe

Yasmine's Bizarre View

Welcome to my poem, I'm Yasmine,
Find out about me since I'm breathtaking!
I adore vanilla ice cream,
But chocolate boosts my self-esteem.
I'm a fan of walking,
But who said I don't like talking?
I have a heart of gold,
Which makes me feel bold!
Sometimes I don't feel alive,
But I still call myself a funny phantom!
I am as fast as a lightning bolt,
And I'm as radiant as diamonds in the sky on a sunny day.
I like my Pepsi how I like my ice cream,
Chilled and fresh.
When I'm excited,
Even a knock will give me a shock!
I always feel joyful with my friend,
That sometimes I never want it to end.

Yasmine Aly Wahba (11)
Millbrook Combined School, High Wycombe

A Poem All About Me

This is a poem all about me,
So please keep reading, hear my plea.
I like eating ice cream,
But I don't like hearing a scream.
Sometimes I feel lame
But I know that soon I'll have a lot of fame.

I love chocolate,
But when I can't find it, I feel unfortunate.
I'm as fast as a cheetah,
But it doesn't mean I am a cheater.
Thai sweet chilli is the best,
Flaming hot puts my mouth to the test.

When I start running, I am one with the ground,
When I play hide-and-seek, I am never to be found.

Now that you know all about me,
Write your own and it might go down in history.

Hassan Qureshi (10)
Millbrook Combined School, High Wycombe

All About Me

I'm a very kind person and very joyful,
I like to eat cake but I also like to bake my favourite food,
What about you?
My favourite chocolate is Galaxy chocolate
And I have it in my room,
I like to eat chicken because it's finger-lickin',
I also like jellies and I have a cat called Kelly,
It has big crystal, shiny eyes.
When it's hot and sunny
I always have a swimming pool ready
But when it's cold and icy
I always have a bathtub ready and warm.
I like to travel to London
Because it has the best theatres.
I also like to go to Birmingham
Because it has the best food I have ever had.

Muhammad Ayaan Qureshi (10)
Millbrook Combined School, High Wycombe

Dream Day

My favourite buttery glazed pancake,
Floating on a chocolatey delicious lake.

I open my brown creaky door,
Walking through the first glistening snow.

Examining a rigid, rough, red rose,
Standing straight, giving a cute pose.

Harry Potter whizzing through,
May I have a ride on your huge fluorescent shoe?

The breeze of the airy sky,
Fulfils my painful aching heart, reminding me
of home.

My huge fluorescent shoe,
Falls down from the sky that's blue.

I stringently rub my eyes where it seems
I'm ruining my wonder and lovely dreams.

Shriyuthika Ramesh Dhayanand (10)
Millbrook Combined School, High Wycombe

Dream Day

For breakfast, I have an awesome eclair sundae
and a toffee milkshake.
While I eat, the sun shines soulfully on the
swimming pool.
I share my dream day with my cute little brother,
Adarsh.

We both like dancing in Britain's Got Talent.
We draw in a giant, supercool spaceship.
24 legendary actors act with me as we dance
gracefully.
The soundtrack is 'Raining Watermelons'.
When I get into my cosy, warm bunny print
pyjamas I have a cup of warm hot chocolate with
marshmallows.
I get to sleep on a fluffy, giant, white cushion, yay!

This is my dream day!

Swetha Elumalaiyan (10)
Millbrook Combined School, High Wycombe

This Is Me

This is a poem all about me,
Please don't ever make fun of me.
I love ice cream but not mushy peas,
Whenever I'm down
I never ever frown.
I'm as bright as the sun,
I always love to have some fun.

I am as skinny as a stickman,
Thai sweet chilli is my game,
My fabulous work is never lame.
I am as tall as a giant,
I am perfect and memorable.
I love chocolate,
Whenever I find it I feel fortunate.

I always do my best,
Because I'm better than the rest.
I live in a town
Because I'm not a clown!

Maleha Ghauri (10)
Millbrook Combined School, High Wycombe

How To Make Timotei

First, you need 2kg of humour.
Make sure it is Messi (Lionel Messi)
So it can score the goal.
Bake in the oven for twenty minutes.

Take out of the oven and pour in phones.
Add in one console so it can play.
Five scoops of Quality Street would be sweet.
A few puppies added will make it bark.
And add a few Lambos so it can run.
Put in a football and kick into the oven.

After it cools down,
Top off with gems so that it can sparkle,
And jets so it can fly.
A satisfying feeling down your throat.

Timotei Blindu (10)
Millbrook Combined School, High Wycombe

My Daily Life

I wake up in the morning,
Get out of bed.
Just to let you know,
My favourite colour is red.
I go to my desk
With my shadow grey pencil.
Then I go shopping
To buy a new stencil.
I live on Plumer Road,
Not that far from school.
Every time I look at ice cream,
It makes me drool.
I am on my desk,
With my mate,
Doing some drama drawing
Of a great gate portrait.
I am as quiet as a mouse
And as careful as a cat
Whenever I draw a picture
Of a big magic hat.

Lawrence Pop (11)
Millbrook Combined School, High Wycombe

How To Make Lucas

A sprinkle of luck
Because I'm lucky like a four-leaf clover.
12g of unique powder
Because I'm unique like everybody else.
2kg of creativeness
Because I'm creative like Picasso.
A tbsp of energy
Because I never run out of energy.
A tsp of enthusiasm
Because I'm enthusiastic.
A bucket of sports
Because I'm as sporty as Ronaldo.
A mix of loudness
Because I'm as loud as a booming elephant.
Then stir it up.
Now you should have a Lucas.

Lucas Wharton (11)
Millbrook Combined School, High Wycombe

Monkey Man

Friend to the chitter-chattering, marvellous,
Magnificent monkeys, apes and chimpanzees,
Works at a place with wonders untold,
But what is his name?

He looks after the orphaned monkey and his children
Until one of their kind is found.
The monkeys are his job,
His friends and family,
But what is his name, can you tell me?

All the way in Dorset
But his name's still a mystery.

I guess we'll never know the mystery monkey man.

Stevie Avery (11)
Millbrook Combined School, High Wycombe

What Do You Know About Ella?

Hey everyone, listen yo!
Gonna tell you some stuff you need to know.

A ball of rhythm,
A ball of text
And a ball of fun,
That equals me.

Add paws of dogs too,
Don't forget the dance,
Add some drums for the beat.
Oh wait, I just remembered,
That equals me.

Don't forget the kindness
'Cause it's key.
And you can't spell
'Awesome' without me!
A ball of rhythm
And that equals me!

Ella Guy (10)
Millbrook Combined School, High Wycombe

How To Make Priya

Find a bowl as big as a lion's head,
Add the first 2 cups of silliness,
Mix in some flour,
Stir it just right.

Find another bowl and sprinkle the sweet sugar,
Pour in 2 bowls of Lithuania,
Add some pandas too!
3 cups of fun and a dash of silliness.

Stir it together
And add it into the giant bowl.

500g of intelligence,
355g of braveness
And 2 tiny tsp of laziness,
Stir it up for the last time
And this is me!

Priya Palaniappan (10)
Millbrook Combined School, High Wycombe

My Garden

My eyes can see ruby-red roses dancing in
the wind.
My eyes can see the tallest apple tree in
the garden.
I can see the gentle grass touching my fingers.
I can feel the petals of the flowers.
I can taste the sweetness of the large apple.
I can taste the juice in the tomatoes.
My ears can hear the bees buzzing.
My ears can hear the birds singing.
The scent of daisies fills my nose.
The smell of fresh apples fills my nose.

Ellie-Jane Peacock (10)
Millbrook Combined School, High Wycombe

All About Eshal

T all as a tree and as beautiful as can be.
H er hair dances in the air as she walks downtown.
I nspires people to draw and never gives up.
S trong, smart, sophisticated like a lioness.

I ntelligent and bold.
S he's as graceful as a peacock.

M agnificent and brave like a horse, *neigh!*
E shal is as elegant as a swan in the lake.

Eshal Kayani (10)
Millbrook Combined School, High Wycombe

My Personality

If you want to know about me,
Then have a cup of warm tea.
So sit down on that chair right there,
Let me start this fair and square.

I'm as kind as a goddess,
I don't really stress.
I'm friendly like a buddy,
I'm as playful as a monkey.

I'm as quiet as a ghost,
I know what I do the most.
My favourite food is toast,
I'm as deaf as a post.

Sesali Wijerathne (10)
Millbrook Combined School, High Wycombe

All About Me Song

Hey you, yeah you, listen to me
I gonna tell you stuff about me
If you're interested listen to this song
Do you know my name?
My name is Khadija
I love to write and sing
When you need help look for me
And tell me your problem
And I will try and make you happy
With words like you're a diamond
A gem and a star
You might like me as a friend
You might not like me.

Khadija Basharat (10)
Millbrook Combined School, High Wycombe

All About Crazy Craig

I play Xbox games more than anything else.
I don't go a day about surfing online.
My technological brain craves the mechanical part there-of.
My favourite game is Rocket League
Because so many people play a part.

Things I dislike are art, bullies and Internet trolls.
They make me want to break my monitor.
They do not tear me apart like a piece of paper
For I am Crazy Craig!

Craig Attafua-Simmons (11)
Millbrook Combined School, High Wycombe

How To Make Zaina

First, add 3 tbsp of energy,
Add 2 litre of jokes,
Add 7 cups of creativity,
Stir for 10 seconds,
Then add 6 tsp of sugar,
3 cups of laughter.

What have you got so far?

Add 10 litres of fun,
1 pinch of silliness.

Nearly there!

Add 750g of flowers
And last but not least
1000ml of kindness.
Sit back and enjoy me shine.

Zaina Fazal (11)
Millbrook Combined School, High Wycombe

Jemima

Jemima
Is kind and thoughtful.
Jemima
Is like Harry Potter.
Jemima
Is sweet.
Jemima
Is fabulous (good at fashion).
Jemima
Is good at maths.
Jemima
Loves art.
Jemima
Is good at drawing.
Jemima
Is 10 years old.
Jemima
Wants a brother.
Jemima
Hates spiders (especially black widows).

Jemima
Is just a human.

Jemima Hamer (10)
Millbrook Combined School, High Wycombe

My Dream Day

For breakfast, it's triple chocolate fudge
But the football cake would not budge.

The snow slowly settled
And the acorns rattled.

Curly cat was purring on the snowy lane
And I was drawing a lion's mane.

24 footballs to kick,
The ground the dogs are starting to lick.

Sleeping with a thousand footballs,
I am writing in a bundle.

Pavit Pradhan (9)
Millbrook Combined School, High Wycombe

Tall As Two Trees

T all as two trees, that's what I am,
H ealthy as a bodybuilder, that's me.
I ncredibly fast, I'm like Usain Bolt,
S ilent as a ninja, that's who I am.

I mpressive, that's what I am,
S tealthy, that's me.

M anners is something I'll always have,
E mphasising my talents, that's me.

Muhammad Ali Khan Bangash (10)
Millbrook Combined School, High Wycombe

All About Saara Mahmood

T all as a window and lovely as a magnificent Muslim.
H elpful as a monkey, chatter, whoop, ooh-ooh ah-ah.
I ntelligent as Albert Einstein.
S tudies for school.

I s an efficient student.
S he has light brown, bright, brilliant hair.

M arvellous as a parrot,
E xcellent as a student of Millbrook Combined School.

Saara Mahmood (10)
Millbrook Combined School, High Wycombe

Flash Farhan

Today I am talking about me,
I think you are lucky.
Well, let's talk.
I'm Flash Farhan and I am fast,
Fast as Sonic.
I'm light as a feather,
Oh, it's a great time to run,
Look at the weather.
I like football, it's astonishing
And I pass like there's no forever.
And when I score I roar,
I'm the best
And I never rest.

Farhan Hanif (10)
Millbrook Combined School, High Wycombe

How To Make Me

You will need 3 jugs of happiness
And 4 cups of laughter.
You will need 2 tbsp of laziness
And 3oz of craziness.

10 pinches of respect
And a few cups of enthusiasm.
2 tsp of light,
100ml of silliness is just right.

5 bowls of sweetness
And 1000g of love.
250g of creativity.
Last but not least,
You will need 3 cups of curiosity.

Rumaysah Akbar (11)
Millbrook Combined School, High Wycombe

Art Is Cool

A little art class can change you.
R unning late for each class.
T urning up at the same time.

I *can't miss this*, you say to yourself.
S houting at your parents to get you there.

C losing the car door,
O pening the gate.
O pening the door,
L ooking at your masterpiece.

Qudsia Rasheed (10)
Millbrook Combined School, High Wycombe

All About Mehwish

T all as a giraffe and gorgeous as can be.
H elping is her hobby.
I s an artistic lion, *roar, growl, hiss!*
S mart, strong, sophisticated like a fox.

I nspiring as Albert Einstein.
S he has soft black hair that jumps in the air.

M agnificent like a cat.
E nergetic kitten is who I am!

Mehwish Kamran (10)
Millbrook Combined School, High Wycombe

How To Make Me

10 lb of angel and devil.
A pinch of shy, maybe a little more than a pinch.
Sprinkle of funny possibly, but not more than
3 drops.
15 lb of scared of spiders or a little more.
2 chocolate chips for my eyes but really dark.
1 ml of cuteness.
Lots of mls of friendly and I mean it.
15 lb of lazy, or just a little more.

This is me!

Rameen Kaleem (9)
Millbrook Combined School, High Wycombe

This Is The Life Of Cheyenne

I'm beautiful caring Cheyenne,
I'm always being helpful even at home,
I can do anything you like but not bad things,
I have really good friends and they're really helpful,
I'm always working hard every day,
I have sisters but they are really annoying,
I like food but not a lot though,
My teacher is cool who I really like.

Cheyenne Mauger-Garraway (11)
Millbrook Combined School, High Wycombe

This Is Me

S weets and science are my favourite things.
A pples are healthy and give me energy.
V acations are my favourite time.
A pril is the month I was born.
N ever give up is my motto.
N othing can stop me.
A rtistic talent runs through my veins.
H appy smile is always on my face.

Savannah Davies (8)
Millbrook Combined School, High Wycombe

Emaeli

E maeli is what I was named.
M y dog is what my dad tamed.
A niyah is my best friend.
E aster is my least favourite day when the Easter bunny left.
L oving autumn vibes, all the red and orange leaves flowing through the breeze.
I love colours on umbrellas, raindrops falling on my knees.

Emaeli Bowring (8)
Millbrook Combined School, High Wycombe

How To Make Alessia

2½ tsp of laughter,
5 pinches of sugar,
4¼ cups of clumsiness,
9 cups of creativity,
6 cups of respect,
Mix until anime bubbles start to burst,
10 tsp of fun,
2½ dashes of joking around,
2 tsp of sportiness,
And the last ingredient
Is 1000ml of energy.
Sit back and enjoy.

Alessia Maita (11)
Millbrook Combined School, High Wycombe

This Is Me

I am amazing Alessia,
Who can sing like Sia.
I am always trying my hardest,
In every single test.
You'll never see any mess,
Or untidiness.
I am kind and caring
And always sharing.

I always tell the truth
And I am never rude.
I am faithful
And careful,
For this is who I am.

Alessia Petrescu (10)
Millbrook Combined School, High Wycombe

Me

I am kind and caring,
Also fantastic at sharing.
I'm cool like school
And always follow the rules.
I'm as calm as a sleeping cat
But I hate rats.
I can't run many laps
But I can read maps.
My name is Theo,
My best friend is Rio.
I like cats
Because they help get rid of rats.

Theo Phillips (10)
Millbrook Combined School, High Wycombe

A Boy Called Jayden

Jayden my name is,
The boy who likes walking in high vis.
My Rubix cube shines bright
Under the starlight.
I like to play with it in class
Or outside on the grass.
I have a cat named Mia,
She has a friend called Leah.
They enjoy knocking down my cactus plants
And annoying the ants.

Jayden John (10)
Millbrook Combined School, High Wycombe

How To Make An Alacia

15g of energy
1 tsp of kindness
1 sprinkle of creativity
1 drop of happiness
6g of care
A mix of luck

You'll need...
Energy, kindness, luck, creativity,
Happiness and care.

Lastly, stir it all up
And you should have a creative, careful
And kind Alacia.

Alacia Robinson (10)
Millbrook Combined School, High Wycombe

My Cake

To make a perfect cake put in messy flour.
For the sweetness, pour a cup of silly sugar.
Bake for four hours and then take it out.
Don't let it cool down and cover it with
fearless icing.
Let it cool for 24 hours.
When cooled down put a pinch of humour.
Serve it on an awesome plate.

Harjot Singh Sidhu (10)
Millbrook Combined School, High Wycombe

All About Afia

Hello everybody, this is me, what's my name?
Afia, and I'm ready for a game.
I'm a fashionista, just wanted to let you know,
Run to get jewellery, always on the go.
Reading is my thing,
Need a book? Gimme a ring.
A diamond, a gem, a chocolate bar,
This is me, I am a star.

Afia Ali (10)
Millbrook Combined School, High Wycombe

All About Me

Hello, my name is Hafsa,
I am fun, friendly and have a flair for acting,
You would want to be friends with me,
I have a golden heart!

Add a tsp of enthusiasm,
A bucket of annoyance,
A cup of helpfulness
And a pinch of reading,
Then mix them together
And this is me!

Hafsa Ajaz (10)
Millbrook Combined School, High Wycombe

This Is Me

T iny is my size.
H appy smiles make a happy me.
I ce cream is my favourite.
S inging is one of my hobbies.

I love maths and English.
S chool is my favourite.

M ilk chocolate is the best.
E lephants are lovely.

Hadeeqa Jahanagir (9)
Millbrook Combined School, High Wycombe

How To Make Nikola

Add 3 pinches of laziness,
20 tbsp of Poland,
1005g of energy,
Stir it.
When freckles appear add 3 bowls of kindness,
3 tbsp of silliness,
4 cups of sweetness,
450g of pink sugar,
500g of blue flowers,
And lastly, watch me rise
Up for 30 minutes and enjoy!

Nikola Szydlowska (10)
Millbrook Combined School, High Wycombe

All About Hannah

I like sports, all kinds of sports,
Swimming is my style,
I am curious of maths,
Learning is my jam.

Playing with friends makes me happy,
My favourite games are hide-and-seek and tag.

I am fast like a cheetah,
And like a brave lion that dances in the wind.

Hannah Sampson (11)
Millbrook Combined School, High Wycombe

This Is Me

T his is me.
H air as wavy as a ripple in a lake.
I s a fast runner.
S wimming is my hobby.

I love cats, especially kittens.
S uperfast runner.

M y family is from Risborough and Hull.
E mmie is my name.

Emmie Gorbutt (8)
Millbrook Combined School, High Wycombe

Happy

S ummer is my favourite season.
U mbrellas keep me dry.
M y family makes me happy.
A dverbs are cool words.
I ce cream is the best.
Y ellow is my favourite colour.
A nimals are nice.
H elping is what I like doing.

Sumaiyah-Fatimah Kousar (9)
Millbrook Combined School, High Wycombe

All About Dwellé Carter

As tall as a tree.
As fast as a car.
Is an energetic monkey, saying ah-haa.
Legs like long straight sticks.
Hair like curly fries.
Naughty and a good student
And not the best student in the school.
My name is Dwellé
And I look like my dad.

Dwellé Carter (10)
Millbrook Combined School, High Wycombe

Aaliyah

A nd I love ice cream at the park.
A m a happy rainbow.
L ove making cards with everyone at school.
I 'm a star when I make cards at school.
Y eah, I'm very happy.
A m happy at school.
H ave to be good at school.

Aaliyah Matovu (8)
Millbrook Combined School, High Wycombe

My Feelings

K acee is my name
A pples make me feel healthy.
C ats make me feel warm.
E ating ice cream makes me happy.
E aster makes me joyful.

L ying on my bed makes me tired.
L ong walks make me feel adventurous.

Kacee Longstaff-Lenton (8)

Millbrook Combined School, High Wycombe

This Is Me

T all as a lamp.
H elpful as a mum.
I nteractive all day.
S mart as Albert Einstein.

I am named Hadia.
S trong, smart, sassy.

M agnificent as a flamingo.
E nergetic as a monkey.

Hadia Gulfraz (10)
Millbrook Combined School, High Wycombe

This Is Me

Nadine, that's my name,
Come on now, I ain't playing games.
I like sports,
Yes, that's me.
I'm the most active person on the map,
That is why I'm writing this rap.
That is me,
Can't you see,
That equals me!

Nadine Aakbani (10)
Millbrook Combined School, High Wycombe

All About Me

Hi, my name is Nyla,
I'm kind and respectful,
I like to be supportive,
I love animals,
They make me happy,
I love to bake
An enormous cake.
My favourite animal is a horse,
I'm always trustworthy
And I never lie.

Nyla Riahi (10)
Millbrook Combined School, High Wycombe

Courtney's Acrostic Poem

C aring, crazy, creative.
O nly one of me.
U nique in my own way.
R eady to face any challenge.
T ries hard in anything.
N ever gives up.
E nergetic as lightning.
Y oung and happy.

Courtney Forbes (10)
Millbrook Combined School, High Wycombe

Yurfet

Y ellow is my favourite colour.
U niverse is what we are in.
R eading and rainbows make me rest.
F anta I love to drink.
E nthusiasm is a part of my plan in play.
T ea is the energy I need for the day.

Yurfet Nurhan (8)
Millbrook Combined School, High Wycombe

About Me

Y asmine is a beautiful name.
A ll the candy is sweet to me.
S ummer is the best time for me.
M illbrook is my school.
I ce cream is yummy.
N utella is yummy.
E lephants are cute animals.

Yasmine Matusiak (8)
Millbrook Combined School, High Wycombe

About Me

A ll the people in my class are lovely.
L aughing is my remedy.
I n the swimming pool, I'm a star.
S weets are the best.
S easide is my favourite.
A ll I need is my cake to cheer me up.

Alissa Hancu (8)
Millbrook Combined School, High Wycombe

Football

We like to play lots of video games.
I play football with my friends.
I like to play on my trampoline.
I make people laugh.
I love cats and dogs.
I am as fast as lightning.
I like art.
I love to grow flowers.

Bryan Guedes (8)
Millbrook Combined School, High Wycombe

All About Me

I am funny,
I am giggly,
I am silly,
I am creative,
I am Subhan.
I am wonderful when I behave,
I am clever when I do maths,
I am funny when I tell jokes,
I am kind when I help others.

Subhan Kayani (10)
Millbrook Combined School, High Wycombe

Happy

H appy days come along
A nd everybody sings a song.
P urple is the colour of my uniform.
P earl shines bright in the morning sky.
Y ellow is the colour of my French fries.

Rumman Kanwar (8)
Millbrook Combined School, High Wycombe

Jay's Rap

Hey everyone, my name is Jay,
I am so cool I don't have to pay,
I can easily run away,
See me at the park,
I've been running all day,
Wake up, win all of the races,
Everyone chases.

Jayden Garvey (10)
Millbrook Combined School, High Wycombe

How To Make Me

You will need 100ml of perseverance.
A pinch of silliness.
2 litres of sportiness.
150ml of kindness.
With a mixture of madness,
A pinch of happiness
And a litre of leadership.

Kaitlin Slatter (10)
Millbrook Combined School, High Wycombe

All About Archie

I am Archie,
I like books with good looks,
I'm also amazing at making bracelets.

I am kind,
My favourite animals are, of course,
A dog, lion and a cat.

Archie Champneys (10)
Millbrook Combined School, High Wycombe

I Am Wonderful

I am wonderful when I do my work.
I am clever when it's math.
I am funny when I am on the playground.
I am kind when I help my mum.

Azaan Azad (11)
Millbrook Combined School, High Wycombe

Tavia

T alented,
A rtistic,
V ery fast as running,
I ncredible,
A mazing,

N ailed it!

Tavia Ndudzo (10)
Millbrook Combined School, High Wycombe

This Is Me

I'm good at football.
I'm good at cricket.
I'm as short as a Year 5.
I'm 10 years old.
I'm Rayan.

Rayan Kanwar (10)
Millbrook Combined School, High Wycombe

Happy Land

Anger and sadness lives in the deepest places
But anger always gets to me,
No matter what it won't go away
So I just take a deep breath in and a deep
breath out.
Love, cuddles and kisses always fix the anger.
Now I just relax, play, talk and fly away.
The creation I dream is always the win,
I seek, I peek but I know it will always be okay.
Now I'm so happy I go into my imagination
And the name is Happy Land.
In Happy Land, all my friends are there
So all we do is ride on giant hamsters
Named Chocolate and Cookie.
When we go to bed we sleep on tie-dye unicorns.

Elliot Haynes-Ward (9)
Ripley Junior School, Ripley

My Dragon Daydream

In my daydream, I am a light blue dragon.
I fly amongst rainbows and I live underwater.
Sometimes I go to Candyland, it's not far from
my cave
But sometimes when I'm in a rush and I take
a shortcut,
I don't very often go through Nightmare Land.
I breathe fire when I hear about the nightmares
that children have.
I also rescue ponies, they are my pets,
They live above my cave
Because they can't live underwater sadly.
I eat candyfloss and my best friend is an octopus.
Anyway, I have to go, do visit again though.

Ella T (9)
Ripley Junior School, Ripley

Who I Really Am

This is the inner me,
The one with an unstoppable imagination.
I can understand your feelings,
Emotions and problems.
I get so deep into a book, I simply cannot stop.
I'm the one with the power
To thrive amongst my wildest dreams.
If I see someone alone
Or looking sad or angry
I ask them if they are okay.
I'm caring, I'm patient
And I'm always here to help.
I run if I hear someone yelp.
Some people as well as you
Might think I'm lonely and unhappy
But the inner me is who I really am.

Annabel Brown (9)
Ripley Junior School, Ripley

My Daydream

When I finally get out of reality,
I ride on my pet dragon on top of Dragon Land's mountains.
I go through portals into Candy Land,
Beach Land or even Winter Land,
But Nightmare Land is the worst.
It makes all your worst nightmares real,
Like the devil, a monster
Or even an evil gingerbread man.
But Dragon Land's school is the best,
You get to ride your own dragon
And become a superhero or a pro at the dragon games,
I love this place but I love my real home more.

Daisy Hinett (9)
Ripley Junior School, Ripley

Sadness

Sometimes I get sad, mad, curious, joyful, glad
But mostly, I get sad.
It could be because of family problems,
Being called names and much more!
A way to fix your problems
Is to hug something or someone.
Think about the problem,
Cry if it's needed or wanted,
Try to show your feelings if possible,
Take deep breaths
Until you're ready to talk about your problems.
This works for me so it might help you.
Sadness will go away for days.

Olivia Walder (9)
Ripley Junior School, Ripley

Things That Make Me Happy

My cat makes me happy,
He's so soft and cute.
My rabbits make me happy,
They're fluffy and gentle.
My family make me happy,
They're kind and loving.
My teacher makes me happy,
She helps me with my work.

Hide-and-seek makes me happy,
It makes me laugh.
My Xbox makes me happy,
I get to play my favourite games.
My phone makes me happy,
Because I get to text my mum and dad
on WhatsApp.

Corey Hall (9)
Ripley Junior School, Ripley

My Happy Poem

I love being happy,
It makes me smile.
My school makes me happy,
English is the best!
I love being happy,
It makes me laugh.
My home makes me happy,
My tablet games make me relax.
I love being happy,
It makes me feel excited.
My dog makes me happy,
We play and play all day.
I love being happy,
It makes me warm inside.
My family make me happy,
They cuddle all my worries away.

Molly Monks (9)
Ripley Junior School, Ripley

The Unusual Two

A beautiful, black gelding
A phenomenal mare: black head with a grey spotty body and bay bottom.
They were anxious. Scared.
My dream was to do dressage and show-jumping.

It took one month, day by day.
One is Beauty, the other is Pumpkin.

We went to Hoys and Stars.
They both did it and they won!
I am so happy my dream came true.

Isabella-Rose Weightman (9)
Ripley Junior School, Ripley

Games On My PS4 And Xbox

I've got a PS4 and Xbox,
I play on it with friends.
I play Minecraft, Star Wars or FIFA
But my favourite is FIFA
But I love all of them.
Minecraft is a block-based game
And squares and objects.
Star Wars is a common game and film too...
May the force be with you!
FIFA is on my Xbox and it's a football game.

Blake Davis (9)
Ripley Junior School, Ripley

Happiness And Kindness

Happiness lives in the highest places,
Like Heaven or space,
Where many dreams come true.
I smile at strangers,
I challenge myself,
I help out and try new things,
I keep learning, I join in,
I think positive thoughts.
Smile, challenge yourself
And make new dreams.

Max Fletcher (9)
Ripley Junior School, Ripley

Dream In The Sea

Dreams are your imagination,
To ride in the sea,
To wish and kiss, to love and see.
Your imagination will run with you,
Be free in the fishy sea.
In the shell shop, everything is free.
The ocean is blue, just like the sky,
I'm very sad but I've gotta say... goodbye.

Leo Delrosso (9)
Ripley Junior School, Ripley

Sweet Wonder World

Sweet and tangy, sweet and nice,
Sunshine and happiness doesn't give a fright.
Joyful and merry, joyful and merry,
Cheerful and delightful, cheerful and delightful,
I just want to play all day in my sweet wonderland.
I love my sweet wonderland
But I love my real home more.

Poppy Jarvis (9)
Ripley Junior School, Ripley

The Best Of Me

Honesty, kindness and apology,
Determination and trust,
A mind full of triggering questions
And trying to get better day after day
And helping others when they need it most.
Being kind and loyal doesn't cost anything
So always be kind to everyone.

Scarlett-Leigh Starr (9)
Ripley Junior School, Ripley

Happiness

I am happy when I play with my dogs.
I am happy when I go to school.
I am happy playing with my friends.
I am happy when I am with my mum.

I like lots of cuddles
And being at home.
I have lots of family
So I am never alone.

Isobel Waller-Skermer (9)
Ripley Junior School, Ripley

If I Were An Animal

If I were an animal I would be a dog
Because I would have an owner.
I could smell food from a mile away,
I could run ten times faster.
I could drink differently.
Have sensitive hearing
And dig and maybe find treasure.

Ashton Brunt (9)
Ripley Junior School, Ripley

My Dream

My dream started on a fun Thursday night.
In my dream was me as a unicorn,
A majestic unicorn.
I was so happy I felt magic flowing in my horn.
The next thing I knew
I was flying high in the luscious blue sky.

Iona-Lilly Edwards (9)
Ripley Junior School, Ripley

Happiness

Happiness lives in the brightest places
Where laughter and joy shine
And spread around the world.

Being with family,
Playing with friends and gaming,
The listed things make happiness appear.

Joshua Annable (9)
Ripley Junior School, Ripley

Me

I'm nothing special, just little old me
But I try to be the best me I can be.
An actor I wanna be
Sometimes I try to see a future version of me.
Sometimes I can't sleep because of my crazy thoughts
But if you open up and see
I try to be the best me I can be.
I will open up and you can see
I'm lively and free
And I try to be the best me I can be.
My friends say I'm nice and a bit loud,
You can always hear my sound!
To be honest on my first day
I was as quiet as a mouse.
I love acting, it's what I wanna do,
I like pink but I also like blue,
I try to be polite, as polite as I can be,
I wanna be an actor you'll see,
You know what, I'm proud to be me.
I hope you enjoyed this poem

Which is mine now.
Please don't forget,
I try to be the best me I can be.

Clemence Moran-Healy (9)
Sheffield High School For Girls (Junior), Broomhill

This Is Me

P hoebe Mary Doig - This is me!
H opeful that people think I am kind and friendly.
O utgoing and fun-loving, I love my friends.
E veryone thinks I have a wild imagination (sometimes I am away with the fairies!)
B eing creative, making art.
E njoying talking to anyone and everyone about everything.

M y favourite things are...
A lways to be outside swimming, surfing and cycling.
R eading, reading and more reading!
Y omping around the countryside with my dog, Bob.

D reams for the future...
O bserving and protecting turtles - they need our help.
I want to be a marine biologist - I am fascinated by sea life.
G oing to have lots more adventures in the future, I can't wait!

Phoebe Mary Doig (9)
Sheffield High School For Girls (Junior), Broomhill

My Paradise

What's your idea of paradise?
Let me tell you mine,
I'd have cats and dogs and some tame mice.

I would live in a cottage in the hills,
I'll be able to see for miles!
And I'd hear little birds' trills.

There would be walls for climbing,
And paths for running,
And I wouldn't come close to dying!

For in my paradise I would die down,
Watching the sunset as day fades,
And the moon and stars would be like a crown.

It'd have no climate change,
With forests lush and green
And nature everywhere in eyes' range.

What's your idea of paradise?
I have told you mine,
Yours might be different,
And that's absolutely fine.

Julide Senior (9)
Sheffield High School For Girls (Junior), Broomhill

This Is Me

T his is me and I am who I am, no one can change me.
H ere I am, tall not small.
I will never give up and I will always try my best.
S un, rain, lightning or snow, it's always a bright day when I'm on show.

I 'm here, there and everywhere, trying different things, you will never see me sitting in a corner looking grim.
S ometimes being a bit giddy but it never stops me in my tracks.

M ore light than the sun can shine, can you guess who it is? So give them a cheer... It's me!
E nding my acrostic poem remember, you always need a positive attitude and do whatever you want to do.

Orla Hague (8)
Sheffield High School For Girls (Junior), Broomhill

How My Life Goes

I like to study with a buddy.
And at my comforting home
More noise is employed as I play with my toys.
As the day grows I might even groan as I lie in bed
But I wake early instead.
I stretch in the morning,
Right when it's dawning.
Sometimes I play the saxophone though I do it on my own.
I make lots of friends
And it never ends.
I like to read storybooks like little Georgie Cook.
Sometimes I make my voice low
So I keep on and go.
I play all day in the sun's rays,
When I go to school it's very cool.
As the sun sets I start to rest.

Ava Rogers (7)
Sheffield High School For Girls (Junior), Broomhill

All About Me

S cience, I like explosions.
U nbelievable, I'm unbelievable but not perfect.
M agic, I can make people happy but not sad.
M aking, I am good at craft.
E xuberant, I am very exuberant and bubbly with laughter.
R esilient, I love to keep trying.

K ind, helping people in need.
E mpty, people should never have an empty heart.
L oving, love your family the way you love yourself.
L iking, like people the way you like yourself.
Y ummy! I do like my food.

Summer Kelly (9)
Sheffield High School For Girls (Junior), Broomhill

This Is Me

This is me,
As brave as can be.

I do stumble
But do not mumble.

Instead, I reflect,
Take a deep breath
And make it a part of my dance.

I may not be the finest,
But I put it to the test.

When I can't do something,
I never give up,
And try to be the best of me I can be.

I challenge myself,
And strive hard for success.

I always face the sunshine,
And the shadows fall behind me.

So this is me
And I can be who I want to be.

Aanya Saxena (10)
Sheffield High School For Girls (Junior), Broomhill

All About Me, You'll See!

This is me and I like to be funny
When the day is sunny.
I have short hair and I like to share.
You see, I have brown skin
And I don't play the violin.
I have black eyes
And I really like fries.
I like jeans but I hate green beans.
One of my hobbies is to sing
But running is not my thing.
I enjoy dance
And my favourite place to go is France.
I am quite smart
And I like chocolate tarts.
I am kind,
If you lose something I will help you find.
As you see, this is me.

Pranathi Naveen (8)
Sheffield High School For Girls (Junior), Broomhill

As I Ride

As I ride through the meadow,
The wind in my hair,
I breathe in the crisp morning air,
The rhythmic sound of hooves going *clip-clop, clip-clop!*
Why would I ever need to stop?

As I ride on for miles,
Not a care in the world.
My horse gets spooked and off I get thrown!
I sit down and cry, wishing I was at home.
I cry so much, I lull myself to sleep,
Then I open my eyes and stretch out my feet,
As far as downstream,
And I realise, it was all but a dream.

Ariana Ramlakhan (9)
Sheffield High School For Girls (Junior), Broomhill

My Style Is Unique

Wavy black hair and chocolate brown skin,
I would rather be in the light than in the dim.
I came across my emotional feelings -
Happy, sad and scared.
I am very passionate about plants and trees out there.
I am very good at maths but better at English.
I am as kind as a dove to my friends
And I am unique,
I achieve many certificates as I try my best,
And help a friend and do my best.
I am very friendly to my family, friends and so are they.
Everyone is unique and so am I.

Neha Varghese (9)
Sheffield High School For Girls (Junior), Broomhill

The Awesome Me

This is me.
I am silly every day
Anywhere all the time.
And I am messy
Don't clean up after I make a mess,
Unless I'm at someone's house that is not
my house.
And I am kind to everybody I want to be
Like my friends and family.
And I am fun to play with when I'm happy
Like everybody should be.
I am friendly
If you are nice to me.
I am courageous at school all day
Every day like I should be,
I am awesome all the time
And I love being me.

Matilda Wild (9)
Sheffield High School For Girls (Junior), Broomhill

What I Am Proud Of

I am proud of having a lovely, kind family.
I am proud that I have a loyal friend.
Well, I am proud of myself because I am very creative
And also so kind to others!
I am myself because I act myself!
Always be yourself as well
And never change.
Also, I am happy to have two kind, generous teachers.
This is me.
I am proud because I am positive of others.
This is me because I am friendly, loyal,
Incredible, brave and encouraging.
We should all support others and be proud.

Aaruthe Srirakaran (8)
Sheffield High School For Girls (Junior), Broomhill

About Me

Who I am? I am myself.
A girl who loves her family and friends.
Just one girl that's just one thing.
Full of love and kindness and personality,
Just me.
A normal school girl going to school, doing maths,
Oh, that's just me.
Walking long miles with my dog, Dolly,
Okay, that's really me.
Loving dogs,
Yes, that's me.
Doing my homework,
Yes, that is me.
Being positive.
So if you see me, it's just me!

Trudy Ludlam (8)
Sheffield High School For Girls (Junior), Broomhill

Proud To Be Me

I am a piece of fabric,
With so many different colours.
My colours always change.
Now I'm baby blue,
My creative colour, my kind colour.
I'm also feeling sunny yellow,
My happy colour, my cheerful colour.
I'm feeling a spark of friendly, loving pink,
My favourite colour, my inner colour
And the one that shines out best!
Put them all together and you get me!
A happy person, a free person
And proud to be me!

Isabella Taylor (9)
Sheffield High School For Girls (Junior), Broomhill

All About Me

We are all unique
Some people like soft drinks
Some people fancy pink
Some people can't wink
Who are you?
Who am I?
That's the question.
Are you a friend who is always there?
Are you a friend who always cares?
Or are you an adventurous girl
Who likes to find pearls?
Who are you?
Who am I?
I'm a soft marshmallow inside
But I am a hard rock outside.
What about you?

Natsumi Wong (9)
Sheffield High School For Girls (Junior), Broomhill

Be Yourself

My soul is bright and beautiful,
I say words that aren't hurtful,
My loving heart as kind as friendship can be,
I'll help my friends and my family help me,
Sometimes I get sad but other times I'm relaxed,
I am calm, gentle and never annoyed,
Everyone is different in all speciality,
Every word you say has individuality,
We all have something to share,
Always by yourself and take care.

Yuge Wang (9)
Sheffield High School For Girls (Junior), Broomhill

This Is Me

T rampolining, gymnastics and horse riding keep me active.
H appy, bubbly and overflowing with energy.
I like doing flips and kicks and silly magic tricks.
S mily, giggly and full of fun.

I always have a messy room.
S leepy in the morning like a sloth bear.

M enorca is my happy place in the sun.
E very day is a new exciting adventure.

Isobel Riddle (9)
Sheffield High School For Girls (Junior), Broomhill

This Is Me Puzzle

Guess what it is...

This thing is unique,
Different in every way.
This thing has facial features
Such as a nose, two eyes and a mouth.
This thing is very adventurous,
Kind or smart or just awesome.
This thing cannot fly
But can dance to the favourite groove.
This thing has its own identity,
Special and personal to them.
What is it?

Answer: It is you!

Sara Nasim (10)
Sheffield High School For Girls (Junior), Broomhill

The Funny Honey

I am funny
I like to eat honey
I like to go out when it is sunny.

I am smart
I like so much art
I love my friends from my heart.

I am eight years old
And I am bold
And I like to wear a necklace made from gold.

I like to run
And I love to have fun
And play drums in the sun.

My dreams are endless
I will always be fearless.

Habiba Gabr (8)
Sheffield High School For Girls (Junior), Broomhill

Who Is It?

She has perfect peach skin.
She has big brown eyes.
She has short, dark brown hair.
She has cherry-red lips.
She has short brown eyebrows.
She has boingy legs.
She has a big smile with lots of teeth.
She has a scary frown when she wants to.
She has a comforting smile.
She has rosy-red cheeks.
She has silly, funny humour.
Who is she?

Answer: Me!

Mimi Taylor (7)
Sheffield High School For Girls (Junior), Broomhill

This Is Me

A dream is like a seed you care for
Nurture, water and be there for
I want to be an Olympian one day
Standing on a podium with my medals on display.

Small steps I must take
For that dream, I will make
This journey will be fun
With adventures yet to come.

My vision is clear
As the Olympics draws near
My goal will be met
And the gold I will get.

Isabella Cancello (10)
Sheffield High School For Girls (Junior), Broomhill

All About Me

Good eyes for reading
Dark hair for smartness
Big mouth for talking
Large ears for listening
Strong legs for running
Kind heart for caring
Green fingers for gardening
Strong arms for swimming
Great humour for jokes
Nice voice for singing
Good creativity for art
Hatred for rice pudding!

Anya Mangat (8)
Sheffield High School For Girls (Junior), Broomhill

Ode To Life

My life is fun,
My life is happy,
I would like a day that isn't yappy!
My life is exciting
Even when I'm bored.
I love life, and that's no fraud!
I love maths and my friends who make me laugh.
I may get distracted but I love to practise.
Now that's me done, tell me about you!

Lilia Maraqa (10)
Sheffield High School For Girls (Junior), Broomhill

I Am Isabelle

I am Isabelle
S o I can be me
A re you kind because I am
B ut if you make me angry I can box
E ven though I only had one term of training
L et me work in peace and then I will
L earn new things as years go on
E ven though I'm Isabelle.

Isabelle Flemons (9)
Sheffield High School For Girls (Junior), Broomhill

This Is Me

Stunning blue eyes for gazing.
Light brown hair for hairstyles.
Large mouth for talking.
Long legs for running.
Strong arms for swimming.
Lots of freckles for cuteness.
Steady hands for art.
Big brain for ideas.
Loud voice for cheering people on.
This is me.

Carlotta Bailey (8)
Sheffield High School For Girls (Junior), Broomhill

That's Why I'm Me

I'm me and that's all I really have to say,
When I play I'm funny and I love to eat honey.
I'm fearless, I guess unless I see a spider I freak
And hide under my bed until I am dead!
My favourite thing to do doesn't apply to you.
That's why I'm me.

Amelia Somasundram (8)
Sheffield High School For Girls (Junior), Broomhill

Who Am I?

I ncredibly proud, determined and true

A mbitious, risk-taking, strives for gold
M otivated, inspiring, active and kind

M ature, responsible and trustworthy
E mpathetic, friendly and warm.

Who am I?
And who are you?

Riha Ganesh (11)
Sheffield High School For Girls (Junior), Broomhill

Me

Hi, I'm a smart girl,
One of the only people that like English
and maths.
I am good at swimming and gymnastics.
A topic that we're learning about is space -
Saturn, Mars.
I'm also helpful and awesome.
Who am I?

Answer: Me.

Alicia Villalba Ramos (8)
Sheffield High School For Girls (Junior), Broomhill

I'm Friendly

F ull of happiness and hope.
R eading is enjoyable.
I like to eat sushi.
E nergetic and enthusiastic.
N ice to people.
D rawing is amazing.
L iving with my family is fun.
Y ou can achieve anything.

Amelia Beck (9)
Sheffield High School For Girls (Junior), Broomhill

This Is Me

This is me
And I will always be
I always include
My favourite food is meatballs
And my goals
Are to always work hard
I like making cards
My favourite subject is maths
It's a blast
Well this is me
Is this who I want to be?

Anu Akilan
Sheffield High School For Girls (Junior), Broomhill

About Me

This person is helpful and kind,
She has lots of ideas in her mind,
She is also jolly and a bit jiggly,
She is a tiny bit silly and very giggly,
She likes to swim and play,
She likes to grin all day.
Who is this?

Answer: Me!

Emma Kong (7)
Sheffield High School For Girls (Junior), Broomhill

The Best Life Of Me

I'm very energetic,
It feels like I have springs in my feet.
I like to run around and play
With other children on my street.
I like to talk and chatter
With everyone around.
I like to play in the rain
When it goes pitter-patter.

Phoebe Preston (7)
Sheffield High School For Girls (Junior), Broomhill

Acorns

Like an English oak tree,
My life was grown from a seed,
Flown here on the wind,
To be the trunk for the branches of my family.
Sometimes it's complicated to say how I was created,
More often, I'm proud of being uniquely me.

Kitty Sumner (9)
Sheffield High School For Girls (Junior), Broomhill

My Acrostic Poem

F orever together.
R elationship matters.
I nclude everyone.
E quality matters.
N ever betray.
D ifference doesn't matter.
S tay together forever!

Aleesha Pillay (8)
Sheffield High School For Girls (Junior), Broomhill

This Is Me

I am brave
I am always friendly
I am kind and caring
I am determined to face my fears
I am unique
I am a person who never gives up
I am a hard worker
I am all this and more.

Noor Akram (10)
Sheffield High School For Girls (Junior), Broomhill

This Is Me

I have a dog and he is so cute,
Even when he is in his suit,
He can jump as high as a kite,
Or maybe even a little higher,
He's my fluff but he's not tall,
So the perfect size to snuggle you,
You sometimes he gets in a little bubble,
But still, he is great to snuggle,
He is not as big as the Eiffel Tower,
But sometimes he is louder.

I am short and blonde,
My eyes are blue, bluer than the sky,
I'm not that tall but not that small,
You look at me, I look at you,
I love my family and love my friends too,
My favourite animals are dogs and horses.

This is my favourite time of the year,
When flowers and poppies appear,
Now you've got to know about me,
Go lay down and rest peacefully.

Bella
St Peter's Church Of England Aided Junior School, Farnborough

Anime Girl

This is me...
I have brown hair with blue eyes,
I'm very tiny in size,
I don't have pets yet,
My favourite food is pasta with pesto,
My favourite drink is Pepsi,
I'm very nosey and caring,
My family says I'm a good therapist,
I love anime, I'm a big fan,
I love reading it, drawing it and watching it,
My favourite dog breed is pugs
Because they have a flat face and wrinkles,
My friends say I'm weird,
My favourite subject is art,
My least favourite subjects are maths and English,
This is me.

Erica Atkinson (9)
St Peter's Church Of England Aided Junior School, Farnborough

Pets Love Me!

My friends say I'm beautiful and kind,
But I don't mind,
I don't like my siblings,
They talk behind my back all the time,
I might be crazy,
Love my family,
Always playing with my pets,
But I am here all the time,
I like to chill and watch movies,
My favourite sport is swimming and netball,
But other people like football,
I used to have eight pets but they all died,
I've got two dogs and a hamster,
They are called Coco, Barney and Riley,
They are really fluffy.

Georgia Taylor (9)
St Peter's Church Of England Aided Junior School, Farnborough

All About Me At School

A rt is my favourite subject
L iteracy is second in line
L anguages are so boring, that includes French.

A fter lunch is the best time of the school day
B ecause then it is nearly the end of the day
O h how I love computing
U nusual, I don't like RE
T errific is going home.

M eanwhile, I love reading Twitch at home
E ventually, I'll end up on the computer gaming.

Jemma Hoare (9)
St Peter's Church Of England Aided Junior School, Farnborough

Me

Talkative mouth for annoying my friends,
Hair is brown just like my eyes,
I like drawing and watching anime as well as dressing up and cosplay,
Sometimes I go on electronics to call my friends
And look up animal facts before my time ends,
I like to believe my friends when they tell me I'm strong,
Still draw even though my friends don't like it,
Mallory is my best friend,
Emma is my name and I hope you like my poem.

Emma Cunningham (9)
St Peter's Church Of England Aided Junior School, Farnborough

Amelia

A nime lover for life, MHA whisperer of the heart is the best
M y favourite sport is horse riding, can't live without it
E ducate at Princes Hall for Stage Coach is enjoyable
L ovely, soft wolves that are very cute and fluffy
I particularly like football, especially being a striker
A mazing Maccy Ds after Stage Coach, I normally have some.

Amelia Lynch (9)
St Peter's Church Of England Aided Junior School, Farnborough

This Is Me

I am a funny bunny lover,
I've got never-ending sea snails, fourteen shrimps,
I just want more!
My favourite food is chickeny chicken,
My favourite drink is Ribena, strong as strong,
My eye colour is blue like the sky
But sometimes it looks grey,
My favourite place to go is the beach,
So no coldness either!
I dislike many foods,
I am a picky eater.

Taya Offord (9)
St Peter's Church Of England Aided Junior School, Farnborough

Georgia

G ymnastics is one of my favourite hobbies
E yes, mine are brown along with my light brown hair,
O 'Connor is my surname
R eading is one of my favourite things to do
G eorgia and Amelia are my best friends
I really love my life and my family a lot
A nimals are something I love too, my favourites are horses and cats.

Georgia O'Connor (9)
St Peter's Church Of England Aided Junior School, Farnborough

This Is Me

I'm a pet lover,
I'm kind and fun,
I'm a Harry Potter movie lover,
My eyes are majestic hazel,
My hair is as brown as chocolate,
I dislike my annoying brother,
I love cooking cakes,
My hero is my mum,
I love being with my friends,
I love Disneyland and Disney movies,
My wish is to go on a Harry Potter tour,
This is me!

Jess Owen (9)
St Peter's Church Of England Aided Junior School,
Farnborough

All About Me, Mallory!

T his is me and I have blue eyes
H appy and smiley
I love plain white noodles
S leep avoider.

I really love hot chocolate
S ometimes with marshmallows and whipped cream.

M e and my friends like my fish, sometimes they bite me
E mma is one of my friends, one of the best!

Mallory Earle (10)
St Peter's Church Of England Aided Junior School, Farnborough

This Is Me

F ootball player
R oblox is my favourite video game
A mong Us lover
N aughty I am not
K id YouTuber reader
I ntelligent
E ater of junk food

B asketball player
U ndertaker 91 is my favourite boxer
R obux spender
G amer
E yes are hazel.

Frankie Burge (9)
St Peter's Church Of England Aided Junior School, Farnborough

This Is Me

I am a little creative
And not that good at colouring or drawing,
My favourite singers are Nikki Minaj and Cardi B,
I have two cats named Carmella and Don,
My best friend's names are Georgia, Sierra, Ellie and Tania,
I really love to cook with my mum,
My sister is called Daisy and I'm Elsie,
This is me.

Elsie-Jayne Slevin (9)
St Peter's Church Of England Aided Junior School, Farnborough

This Is Me

I am a game lover,
I like school,
My colour is mixed,
My favourite animals are dogs and cats,
I am kind,
My friends think I am cool and kind,
Sammy is my best friend,
I love food, games and videos,
I hate school bullies and rude people,
I like pets and teachers like Mr Hudson,
This is me.

Jason Adamik (9)
St Peter's Church Of England Aided Junior School, Farnborough

This Is Me

My name is Georgia,
Horses are my forever,
I despise the big lick,
Cross-country is my thing,
Gallop is my dream,
I am so keen,
Erin is my best friend,
Do you have a problem with that?
Ham on pizza rules,
Pepper drools,
With dogs and cats,
I have described myself!

Georgia Kelly (9)
St Peter's Church Of England Aided Junior School, Farnborough

This Is Me!

T hinks that hockey is great
H eights is my middle name! (Fake!)
I nteresting Isaac is my name
S ometimes I am a pig when eating.

I am speedy like a cheetah
S ea-blue eyes.

M aking things like a busy bee
Eco-.
war
rior

Isaac Morgan (10)
St Peter's Church Of England Aided Junior School, Farnborough

This Is Me

I am a lover of school,
I have blonde hair and blue eyes,
Friendly, nice and caring,
I also love my family and friends,
I like spelling, maths and science,
I dislike climate change and pollution,
I love reading books especially hard ones,
I enjoy cooking and art,
This is me.

Zita L (9)
St Peter's Church Of England Aided Junior School, Farnborough

This Is Me

T iny in size
H ave a mean sister
I love playing with my friends
S wimming is my favourite sport

I love my family and dog
S ometimes we have McDonald's

M y favourite game is Minecraft
E ducation is fun.

Freddie Hankin (9)
St Peter's Church Of England Aided Junior School, Farnborough

This Is Me

T iny in size all the time,
H appy like a holiday,
I love chocolate cakes,
S inging all the time.

I love music,
S illy as a clown.

M usic is the best,
E very day at school I try my hardest.

Evie Churchill (8)
St Peter's Church Of England Aided Junior School, Farnborough

Lucy

L over of animals like snakes, dogs, cats and crocs
U nicorns are not my favourite animal, but I do like horses
C ats are calm and quiet, but dogs are fast and funny, I like them so much
Y eet is my favourite word and I love two-wheeled scooters.

Lucy Grenham (9)
St Peter's Church Of England Aided Junior School, Farnborough

This Is Me

T he bluebell eyes
H e is a sleeping beauty
I am smart
S weetie lover.

I am a chocolate lover
S illy billy.

M y favourite food is sausages
E very animal I love especially rats.

Thomas Anderson (9)
St Peter's Church Of England Aided Junior School, Farnborough

What Is It?

They glide through the sea so swiftly,
They're lazy and sleepy,
They're green and brown with a hint of grey,
They're flat not tall,
They swim through the seaweed with their flippers so thin,
What is it?

Answer: A sea turtle.

James Prinsloo (8)
St Peter's Church Of England Aided Junior School, Farnborough

Who Am I?

E nergetic
R abbit lover
I ndependent
N ice

H arry Potter nerd
A dventurous
M erry
M erit in tap exam
O utstanding friends
N ot normal
D ancer.

Erin Hammond (9)
St Peter's Church Of England Aided Junior School, Farnborough

The Amazing Grace

The amazing Grace with brown puppy eyes,
Who never lies,
Like to sort out her weird shouting out,
An anime reader
Who never listens to her bossy leader,
The curly-haired girl
Who likes to find seashell pearls.

Grace Harrison (9)
St Peter's Church Of England Aided Junior School,
Farnborough

The Biography Of A Penguin-Everyman

I am Sammy,
I like Shawn Mendes,
My sis is stinky,
I look like a pelican,
I like Playmobil,
I don't like making,
I eat chicken McNuggets,
I like memes,
My favourite animal is a penguin.

Sammy Ronald Stembridge (9)
St Peter's Church Of England Aided Junior School, Farnborough

Fantastic Me

I'm a lover of KFC,
I'm also loving, caring and kind,
I'm sometimes not a brave person,
I love dancing a lot,
I sometimes dislike my hair colour,
I love my eye colour,
My hero is my mum.

Freya Sabatini (9)
St Peter's Church Of England Aided Junior School, Farnborough

Me

A kennings poem

I am a...
Comic book reader
Creative drawer
Holiday celebrator
Pet lover
Professional doodler
Excellent drawer
A great friend
A blackcurrant drinker
And...
An awesome gamer!

Gabrielle Wilson (10)
St Peter's Church Of England Aided Junior School, Farnborough

What Animal Am I?

I am slow but not small,
I am furry but not a ball,
I climb like a monkey.
I am very chunky,
I love eating leaves
And hanging on trees,
What am I?

Answer: A sloth.

Felix Thomasius (9)
St Peter's Church Of England Aided Junior School, Farnborough

This Is Me

I am a footballer,
I am a lover of sports,
Strong, resilient and kind,
I am like a lion, happy and quick,
With my glorious eyes
And my ever-changing hair,
This is me.

Liam King (9)
St Peter's Church Of England Aided Junior School, Farnborough

Harry's Inspirational Poem!

A kennings poem

I am a...
Football left winger
Pizza nommer
Hamster lover,
Kind and useful member
Chatty boxer
Holiday lover
Helpful person
Celebrating community member!

Harry Sayer (9)
St Peter's Church Of England Aided Junior School, Farnborough

All About Me

A wesome at English
M arvellous at dancing
E xcellent at singing
L ove all things about horses
I love horse riding
A rtistic mind.

Amelia Gilbert (9)
St Peter's Church Of England Aided Junior School, Farnborough

This Is Me

A kennings poem

I am a...
Dog lover
Chocolate eater
Gaming boy
Football striker
Hot tub lover
Bird hater
Nosey clown
And finally, a silly sausage
This is me.

Callan McGregor (8)
St Peter's Church Of England Aided Junior School, Farnborough

Me

A kennings poem

I am a...
Fortnite lover
Minecraft hater
I like my music
Love my football
Hate veggies
But love my fruit
And finally...
Love the Gunners.

Charlie Dearlove (10)
St Peter's Church Of England Aided Junior School, Farnborough

This Is Me

S mall in height
I ntelligent
D ecorative
D aydreamer
H orses are my favourite animal
I love painting and reading.

Siddhi Pahariya (9)
St Peter's Church Of England Aided Junior School, Farnborough

This Is Me

A kennings poem

I am a...
Book reader
Sushi eater
Winter lover
Animal carer
Food eater
Anime watcher
And finally...
A water drinker.

Filipa Panayotova (9)
St Peter's Church Of England Aided Junior School, Farnborough

I Am A...

A kennings poem

I am a...
Movie lover
Game goer
Football watcher
Food eater
Bad sleeper
And finally...
A Marvel lover.

Riley Harris (9)
St Peter's Church Of England Aided Junior School, Farnborough

This Is Me

I am a lover of PE,
Older, kind and smart,
I am like a tiger, brave and strong,
My cocoa-coloured hair,
This is me.

Tania Isabel Moreira Faria (10)
St Peter's Church Of England Aided Junior School, Farnborough

Favourite Things

A kennings poem

I am an...
Anime watcher
Video gamer
Pasta eater
Dog lover
Football player
And finally,
Tea drinker.

Harley Broom (9)
St Peter's Church Of England Aided Junior School, Farnborough

Always Be Happy

C hristmas is the best time of year
H aribos are my favourite snack
R ice is the best food
I love my family
S our sweets are good
T he very happy monster is happy
M uch kindness
A lways be helpful
S weets are the best.

I ce is good on a hot day
S pring is a season.

N ever ever hurt someone
I love ice cream on a warm day
C an we all be nice
E veryone loves jelly.

Alisa Elabd (9)
Trinity CE Primary Academy, New Park Village

This Is Me

Today may be different
I'll still read with my mind
I'll read day and night
The sun was kind.

Today may be different
I don't feel weird
Except for today, I saw
A man with a weird beard.

Today may be different
Today I'll give space life
Aliens rise from the dead
An alien will come with a knife.

Today may be different
I don't feel dangerous
Once I met a man
Who was nameless.

Today may be different
But I still want to sing K-Pop

I'll sing and sing
Then do a mic drop.

Today may be different
Obviously, I will watch Marvel
But if I am bored
I'll talk to a marble.

Today may be different
I'll run like a sandstorm
While my mouth goes for a ride
I'll be in my bed and be warm.

Today may be different
But babies will still attach to me
I'll go to a hive
I'll hear all the bees.

Today may be different
I'll be very crafty
Maybe I'll open the window
Now it is very drafty.

Nina Saber (9)
Trinity CE Primary Academy, New Park Village

All About Aaron

Roses are red,
Violets are blue,
One day I went to the zoo,
Then I saw a parent that was blue,
Do you know why
Or do you need a clue?

My favourite holiday is Christmas for sure,
All the presents and dinners for fun.
This holiday is definitely number one,
Family come every year,
While everyone spreads the Christmas cheer,
What's your favourite, let's hear!

This is last but not least,
So sit, relax and put up your feet,
This one is really a treat,
This isn't an opinion, it's a fact,
I won't make this long saying this and that,
I like football for sure,
I've been playing since two maybe four,
This is the sport I really adore,

I guess I'm done so don't be shy,
Just wave your hands and say goodbye!

Aaron Haile (9)

Trinity CE Primary Academy, New Park Village

My Determination

I may not be perfect,
But I still try,
My hopes are not raised,
But yet they are high.

I have confidence and resilience,
To put myself to the test,
I will push past my boundaries
To achieve my best.

I am determined
To complete my quest,
I will not admit defeat
And I won't be beaten by the rest.

I will push through
Any obstacles that try to crush me,
I will not relax
Until I am the best I can be.

So this is me,
Like it or not,

Do not judge me,
I will give it my best shot.

Mackenzie Cope (9)
Trinity CE Primary Academy, New Park Village

What Makes Me, Me

As I went to the land of me
The clock struck one
I cook my dog
And I got a burn.

As I went to the land of me
The clock struck two
I went to the toilet
To see my hamster poo.

As I went to the land of me
The clock struck three
I took my laptop under a hive
And got an electric sting from a bee.

As I went to the land of me
The clock struck four
I practised my times tables
Under the shore.

As I went to the land of me
The clock struck five

I fed some milk
To a dangerous beehive.

Ibukun Toye-Akingbola (10)
Trinity CE Primary Academy, New Park Village

How To Have A Good Time

T ruth is the right thing
H appiness is the emotion you should always feel
I am trusted and worthy
S inging is my thing.

I f I annoy people that is wrong
S andra is my best friend ever.

M y favourite thing to do is skipping
Y eah, my favourite thing is pizza.

L ying is the worst thing to do
I am honest and nice
F amous is what I want to be
E llie is my friend.

Ameliah Giles (9)
Trinity CE Primary Academy, New Park Village

How To Bake A Shana Cake!

To create me you will need:
A whole mountain of crazy,
A tub of kindness,
Six big spoonfuls of shyness (or maybe more)
One and a half tablespoons of rudeness.
Three tablespoons of elegance,
A whole jug of loyalty
And you have to be in a clean room,
Stir it all together,
Pop me in a rainbow oven,
Wait for the magic to happen,
A dash of sprinkles and frosting to light up
the place
And display me
Or eat me if that's the case!

Shana Sithole (10)
Trinity CE Primary Academy, New Park Village

Do You Want To Know About Me?

Do you want to know about me?
Well my smile is as big as the sea,
My personality is full of glee,
I'm not as big as a tree,
But if you're looking for a race, I'm free.

Also, I'm lightning on any ball,
A tiny bit small
And a gaming god
And a hater of cod!

I'm a very slick snake,
I have a lot of good mates,
My mind goes beserk without my hobbies,
Finally, this is random but my sister is snobby.

Amit Ozvuke
Trinity CE Primary Academy, New Park Village

Love And Peace

L ove is what counts
O ozy warm hugs
V ests are smart, love is big
E verything in us is peace

A nd peace is what keeps us together
N othing can get between us
D own and over we go

P eace shows everyone has a time to blend in
E asy isn't it, that's not all
A lways show love and peace
C an we do it safe? If we can
E verything can be better!

Tyler Yates
Trinity CE Primary Academy, New Park Village

How To Live My Life

This is how to live my life...

J ust take a deep breath
E veryone is watching you
S elf-confidence is the way
U se your brain
S undae as big as you want
E nter your life and brain
M e and you are here
E stimate about yourself
N ever give up

How to be me
You will need some glee
Take a deep breath
Smile at me
Show me what you need.

Jesusemen Idiakheua (9)
Trinity CE Primary Academy, New Park Village

How To Be Happy Like Me

H appy is my favourite emotion
A sprinkle of happiness is always good
P izza is my favourite food
P astels are good for drawing on black paper
Y oghurt is healthy for me.

I love ice cream
S weets are the best for a bad day.

G old is my second favourite colour
O ld books are interesting to read
O ranges are sweet
D aylight is nice.

Naeemah Adams (9)
Trinity CE Primary Academy, New Park Village

Crazy Animals

As I went down the road
The clock hit midnight
I saw a frog putting in a code.

As I went to the castle
The clock hit midday
I saw a swan eating a pond.

As I went home
The clock hit one
I saw a duck eating a bone.

As I went to bed
The clock hit three
I saw a bee taking selfies.

As I went down town
The clock hit five
I saw a wolf in a hive.

Oliver Blood (9)
Trinity CE Primary Academy, New Park Village

Scared Surprise

For 6 years
I've been scarred with scars
I'm shouting
"Please help me!"

In calling the police
Now you believe the story
They're coming for you
Now you're ranked to number 2.

I'm going out
It's so loud
And I'm still scared
And so I stared.

They arrived
And said, "Hands up and take your mask off."

Malachi Chibwape (10)
Trinity CE Primary Academy, New Park Village

Pinch Of Happiness

Ingredients:
A pinch of happiness
15lb of cheese
Tons of energy
A sprinkle of joy
A toy-filled bedroom

Now you need to:
Put the 15lb of cheese in a tray,
Mix in a toy-filled bedroom,
Add a sprinkle of joy
Then a pinch of happiness,
Put it in the oven for 10 minutes
Then add tons of energy
And leave it to cool down for 20 minutes.

This is me!

Elliott Lees (9)
Trinity CE Primary Academy, New Park Village

Taylor-Jae

T aylor-Jae is my name,
H armanjit is my friend,
I love playing games, riding my bike, and my family,
S our sweets are my favourite thing to eat.

I love football and I like playing with my dad, mom and brother,
S uperman is my favourite thing to watch.

M y favourite thing to do is stay at my nan's
E verybody is nice to me.

Taylor-Jae White (9)
Trinity CE Primary Academy, New Park Village

This Is What I Like...

I like the sun
Because it's very fun,
But there is always rain,
It makes me so mad I can't explain.

I like cats
Because they look so cute in hats,
But I don't like bats
Or rats.

I got a new book
And I like to cook,
But I hate to clean
And I hate beans.

I like games
But I am bad at remembering names,
I love candy canes.

Sabine Zandersone (9)
Trinity CE Primary Academy, New Park Village

Be Strong And Don't Be Scared And Work Hard

Don't be scared
If someone glared.
Be strong, be strong
Work hard for long.
Don't be scared
I just asked because I cared.
Don't even care
If someone doesn't share
Tell them to be fair
Don't even give them a dare.
Just be strong and work out
Don't be scared if they say get out.
Work hard
Never let your head get screwed up like card.

Eashan Kumar (9)
Trinity CE Primary Academy, New Park Village

This Is Me

Today I'm really in the mood for art,
I don't really think I am that smart,
I'm very crafty
But I'm not drafty.

I love sweet food
And I'm in a great mood,
I love the outdoor,
I'm definitely not poor.

I love underwater,
But I can't get smaller,
I'm as kind as a sunflower,
I'm bad at cooking with flour.

Gurroop Kaur (10)
Trinity CE Primary Academy, New Park Village

My Second Favourite Time Of The Year

H alloween is cool but not the best
A ll the sweets are good
L ooking at all the sweets, getting jealous
L oving all the time with my parents
O pening lots of doors
W alking up to lots of houses
E very October 31st it's Halloween
E njoying it, so much fin.
N ot that bad Halloween is.

Michal Martyniuk
Trinity CE Primary Academy, New Park Village

What I Am Like!

T he game called football is very fun
H atred is not a thing in my world
I nquisitive is my type of style
S lick and sly sometimes I can be.

I nstinct is what I always follow
S ometimes I can feel very shallow.

M ysteries are what I like to solve
E nthusiastic is my personality.

Awa Nkengla (9)
Trinity CE Primary Academy, New Park Village

What Ingredients Make Me

A teaspoon of jokes
A pinch of happiness
A jar of hope
A fruit of excitement
A hole of peace
A heart of thoughtfulness
A body of positive behaviour
A ball of playful
World of nature
A life of luck
A good family
Make kindness spread
A stir of red, my favourite colour
Spread of sweetness
A slice of truth.

Uthman Alagangan
Trinity CE Primary Academy, New Park Village

How To Create Nevaeh Pie

You will need:

- A splash of glitter
- A ball of colour
- A dot of happiness
- Sprinkle of dough
- A room full of toys

Steps to create:

First add a sprinkle of dough to a ball of colour, a dot of happiness and mix it.
Put in the oven for 8 seconds, let it cool and sprinkle the glitter on and enjoy.

Nevaeh Anglin
Trinity CE Primary Academy, New Park Village

What Animal Am I?

I am a loyal friend,
I love to play with toys,
I have lots of teddies,
I love food.

I sleep lots,
I am fun to be with,
I have fun with anyone,
I am happy all over.

I love to walk,
I am super fast,
I like to be outside,
Snow and leaves.

Answer: A dog.

Scarlett Walker
Trinity CE Primary Academy, New Park Village

This Is Me

Hey guys my name is Lamaree
And I'm going to take you through all the things about me!
Born in 2012,
Great at gaming,
I bet if you played against me you would lose
And cry which is why I've got a tissue ready,
Great at sport
You can't judge that thought
And that's it for now!

Lamaree Morris-Stewart (9)
Trinity CE Primary Academy, New Park Village

This Is Me

T all as a skyscraper
H ave kindness for everyone
I love being around friends
S hy personality.

I adore singing
S hine as bright as a star.

M arvellous at drawing
E ating food is the best.

Sandra Kriauciunaite (9)
Trinity CE Primary Academy, New Park Village

Bethany

B eing nice to others
E ating all my food
T he work in school, I do all of it
H elping my teacher
A nimals are my favourite
N o hurting other people
Y ounger children are adorable.

Bethany Challenor (8)
Trinity CE Primary Academy, New Park Village

All About Me

A rt is what I like
R iding on my bike
A nd every single day
Y ou remind me what to play
A s time goes by I lie in my bed, use my telescope and look at the night sky.

Araya Robinson (9)
Trinity CE Primary Academy, New Park Village

YoungWriters
Est. 1991

YOUNG WRITERS INFORMATION

We hope you have enjoyed reading this book – and that you will continue to in the coming years.

If you're the parent or family member of an enthusiastic poet or story writer, do visit our website **www.youngwriters.co.uk/subscribe** and sign up to receive news, competitions, writing challenges and tips, activities and much, much more! There's lots to keep budding writers motivated!

If you would like to order further copies of this book, or any of our other titles, then please give us a call or order via your online account.

Young Writers
Remus House
Coltsfoot Drive
Peterborough
PE2 9BF
(01733) 890066
info@youngwriters.co.uk

Join in the conversation!
Tips, news, giveaways and much more!

YoungWritersUK YoungWritersCW youngwriterscw